AF884362

OLIVER AUSTRIA

illustrated by

ALENA TKACH

Phoebe!
Hope you enjoy Odo's Story!
I adore you, little Miss ☺
Keep Smiling
-Oliver

Cool - This is for you too ☺

Copyright 2016 by Oliver Austria

All rights reserved. No part of this book may be reproduced, transmitted,
Or stored in an information retrieval system in any form or by any means,
Graphic, electronic, or mechanical, including photocopying, taping, and
Recording, without prior written permission from the publisher.

ISBN 978-0-9974855-0-9
Printed in California, USA

The most heartfelt gratitude to my incredible partner,
Ms Alena Tkach – you were able to illustrate my thoughts beautifully.

Many thanks to my family:

Tita Sundree, Tita Shamie, Rakesh, Rahni, Rahvin,
Sunill and Lavina, Jag and Ty, Christopher and Brian.

My chosen family:

Jodennie and Rick * Gaella and Tyler * Liza and CJ
Monette and Shawn * Kylie, Khmera and Travis, Lily
Alex and Justin * Nim * Toni Rica * Hal

My TED team:

Morgana, Liz, Jane and Julie.

Printed in California
Ingramspark.com

for Mohnie Olga

Odo is a shy little OWL.

He always wonders
what it would be like
to have FRIENDS.
He feels EXCITED thinking of
all the fun, amazing things
they could do TOGETHER.

This summer,
ODO gets to go to camp
for the FIRST TIME.
He has been looking forward
to the day camp begins
because NOW he has the chance
to MAKE FRIENDS.

The day has finally come,
and Odo is EXCITED!

"JUST BE YOU,"

his mom tells him,

as she drops him off

at the CAMP.

He is determined to meet EVERYONE

and make AS MANY friends

AS HE CAN.

Odo WAVES
at everyone
he sees,
BUT ...
... everyone looks TOO BUSY
meeting each other
to wave back at him.

He takes a DEEP breath
and decides to walk over
to them. "Maybe I should
INTRODUCE myself,"
he thinks.

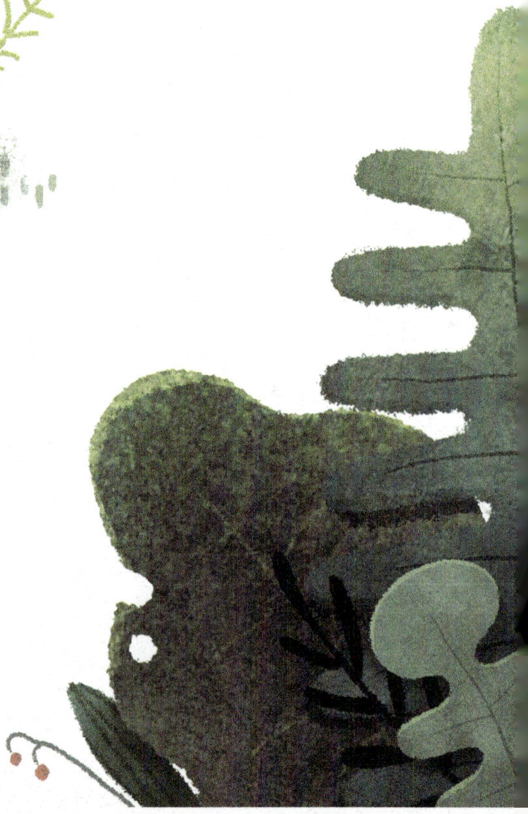

So he walks
to the first group
of CAMPERS
he sees from afar.

Then **Odo** realizes
they are all TOO TALL!
They cannot see him
waving below them.

still HOPEFUL,
ODO moves on
to the next group of birds ...

...and they are all

SO BEAUTIFUL!

Odo feels
OUT OF PLACE.
He is less colorful
than these birds
So he moves on again.

He tries to find his way
through the beautiful feathers,
until he hears
a KNOCKING SOUND.

So Odo follows the SOUND,
walking toward it ...

... and finds himself
in the middle of
an ORCHESTRA!

Or at least
it SOUNDS like one.

All these birds
sing in tune with one another,
to MUSIC Odo does not know.
He tries to add his own melody,
but only one SOUND comes out ...

Hooooooooot...

So Odo walks on again
past the singing birds
and around the CAMPSITE.

He begins to feel like
he DOES NOT
BELONG HERE ...

. . . until he sees
another GROUP of birds
heading to the pond
TO PLAY.

Odo smiles and WAVES ...

... but NO ONE waves back.
The other birds
are TOO BUSY
having fun
to notice him.

Odo had not expected
CAMP to be this SAD.
He had waited SO LONG
for this moment.
He wants so badly
TO BELONG.

It is getting dark,
and the CAMP LEADER
calls all the campers
to the CAMPFIRE.

The OTHER BIRDS
are already gathered by the CAMPFIRE
when Odo arrives.
They are about TO TELL STORIES.

Everyone sits in a circle.

Now it is DARK.

The fire is WARM and BRIGHT ...

... until the WATER BIRDS fly up,
flapping their WET WINGS
and accidentally
PUTTING OUT THE CAMPFIRE.

Suddenly, it is
DARK.

All the campers
are GETTING SCARED.
Some of them start CRYING.
NO ONE can see in the dark,
and NO ONE knows
what to do ...

... except **Odo.**

Odo sees
a box of MATCHES.
He lights ONE and
turns around.
Everyone
is LOOKING AT HIM.

Odo LIGHTS the campfire,
and everyone CHEERS!
All the campers
are relieved and thankful
that Odo CAN SEE
in the DARK.

Finally, Odo makes
lots of FRIENDS!

His MOM was RIGHT, he thinks.
He just needed
TO BE HIMSELF!

Oliver Austria

is a children's author with a fondness for owls and awkward silences.

When not writing - Oliver is a professional figure skater, cutthroat hula hooper and competitive pie eater. Many would say that he wrote this book for the attention, but he admits that it truly is for the children and adults who are young at heart. Oliver is a big advocate of reading and started doing so before he was a year old, around the same time he began his lifelong passion for Alpine yodeling. Oliver is great at telling stories - but not all of them are always true, for instance those in this bio.

He currently resides on the island nation of the Bahamas, where he owns and operates a yak butter farm with his long-term partner, the actor Jake Gyllenhaal.

Alena Tkach

is illustrator from Ukraine. Her work is heavily inspired by nature. Alena is a big fan of foxes, moss and deep forests. She works mostly as children's book illustrator and 2D artist. Alena created her first illustrated book in 2014.

When she is not illustrating for gamedev and publishing clients, Alena likes to hike, taking pictures with a film camera and doing yoga.

CPSIA information can be obtained
at www.ICGtesting.com
Printed in the USA
LVOW05*1906181016
509304LV00012B/19/P

9 780997 485509